Epigraph

The opal and the sapphire of that wandering western sea,
And the woman riding high above with bright hair flapping free—
The woman whom I loved so, and who loyally loved me.

The pale mews plained below us, and the waves seemed far away
In a nether sky, engrossed in saying their ceaseless babbling say,
As we laughed light-heartedly aloft in that clear-sunned March day.

A little cloud then cloaked us, and there flew an irised rain,
And the Atlantic dyed its levels with a dull misfeatured stain,
And then the sun burst out again, and purples prinked the main.

Still in all its chasmal beauty bulks old Beeny to the sky,
And shall she and I not go there once again now March is nigh,
And the sweet things said in that March say anew there by and by?

What if still in chasmal beauty looms that wild weird western shore,
The woman now is—elsewhere—whom the ambling pony bore,
And nor knows nor cares for Beeny, and will laugh there nevermore.

Thomas Hardy

2 Whispers

2 Whispers

GEORGE CARLE

Matador
5 Weir Road
Kibworth Beauchamp
Leicester LE8 0LQ, UK
Tel: (+44) 116 279 2299
Email: books@troubador.co.uk
Web: www.troubador.co.uk/matador

ISBN 978 1848761 391

British Library Cataloguing in Publication Data.
A catalogue record for this book is available from the British Library.

Typeset in 12 pt Bembo by Troubador Publishing Ltd, Leicester, UK

Matador is an imprint of Troubador Publishing Ltd

To my son, Ethan

Contents

A Dream in my Mind

She spoke like a woman
but in my head I saw a child
once dear
but the ague and spirit
had burned my mind
a hundred times since

it took time to know her
the strange dialect
in a woman's body
the empty shell
the times when
she needed me
and I was not there

I felt anguish again
it was like an old friend
returning to haunt me
as an enemy of time
who offered no hope
for the relationship
a dream in my mind.

A Sister Shone Bright

A sister shone bright
in morning town
as daybreak crawled
from horizon's edge

up and up she goes
carrying the spirit
of dead men's dreams

hope lifting love
beyond the reach
of the dreary deed
called death

but the death of love
can never once be sung
the heavens open daily
with rain and summer sun

A Wedding Song

That this dalliance should endure
against all who seek to sway
this time this tide
none shall break

when souls set in romance
worship each and one
none shall come between
this harmony this love

and years may pass
but the sight of love
shall shimmer sweet
this loving this light

Absence Long

Oh it is hard
to bear the loss

the laburnum
with yellow racemes
and seeds of poison

the half grown oak
with rebellious strength
and ageing acorns

nevermore the leaves of
spring the sun of summer
the autumn turn
the bare winter blast

after nurture twin thoughts
kiss lips and breathe hope
where there is none

let me forget
the loving kiss
and absence long.

Aesculus

Old aesculus
trembled and shook
as droplets ran
across leaves
and dripped on to
those below

a swallow flew
out of the canopy
disturbing water
on a hundred leaves
showering dank moss
fifty feet below

creamy white candles
saved from Christmas
softened branches
with no flame
poised for pollination
and nuts to bear.

Ageing Dream

Kiss lightly his name
let songs of life
wander through childhood

watch a boy
creep beyond
a teenage dream

wake him to grasp
adulthood and find
light in his dreams

Ague

Sometimes when the day is long
I look into the head of a dream
the purple mountains of home
where crystal streams caress
the raptured ridge of red
sunlight breathes summer scent
and cool clouds are distant far

then the ague soaks my brain
the red hot beauty of pain
clears my mind and I fall
from cliffs of ageing height
like a leaded feather
my broken body somewhere
beyond age and vigour...

And All Had Been

It was cold that day
as she stood lonely
missing me naked
the nakedness of me

I touched her face
and kissed her lips
but there was no joy
in this world
or nether by

let me go back
I whispered
over and over
as she wept
tears for love
and all had been.

And When it is Over

And when it is over
he will come say
words well spoken
for he is not hate
nor envy nor pain

but dullness will thud
in the heart and mind
and a torrent of curses
will fall from lips

then the over and through
will suck at the mind
until a time comes when
he is naught but a flash
in memory in mind

Autumn Summers Died of Winter Rain

The angel of a boy
I knew no more
his songs were sung
with breath unknown
and the nature of he
once fresh in my ear
now crumbled

by the long walk
of sleeping and waking
the mere fact of life
and its humdrum way
sank silent on me
and autumn summers
died of winter rain

Beating Breath

Let me see old age
the senile moment
the wistful eye
the epiphany of life
that thuds dull
on wish and want

a convoluted curse
separates us from
those who roam and roar

yet we have spoiled;
the rivers run with stench
the seas are full of filth
and global warming waits

where now creator
shall man run his course
and so doing kill
his beating breath

Beauty and the Clawed Beast

Beauty the clawed beast
with blood upon her face
an antelope lies gasping
with bleeding neck to tell

the roaring of a killer
roaring like the rest
bellows to the pride
come feast on frightened flesh

with blood upon their faces
and gore on body more
they rip and tear the carcass
even bones lick hungry sore

the hunter and the hunted
nature all shall tell
about the beast a predator
who hunts and kills so well.

Belately

Belately I say
while purists shall moan
for an added d

it is my way
a way with words
handed with anguish
and weakened mentality

did I hear say
the English bard
did throw in words
were never said before

it surely is a poet
can give them birth
from embryonic elegy
that sings inside his head

Berries

The berries glow sweet
in this their rosy time
when leaves start to fall
and the damper days
cool and cold to winter

they take their kindness
to birds starved on wing
the flesh covers stone
which will pass and fall
to nestle far from parent
a son or queen

oh joy they bring
these berried branches
and then some shall say
what do they bring
if berries be naught
when no birds sing

Crush

She taught him
this woman who gave
fantisies needed
to stir youth

he wondered if she knew

the spice of that day
when she dallied by his desk
to point to a mistake
and brush his hand

over in a second
too much to bear
for tender youth

he laughed years later
to recall this woman
her daughter now his wife

Crust of Comfort Bread

The dead never die
they sit in your mind
and pop up any time
fog blankets the brain

they have no reality
but cycling circuits
give a vivid picture
to frighten reassurance

the naked touch
of those who have gone
to some place else
but still mess you up

sometimes you ask for help
but they never speak
it is after their time
they have no voice

peace is their crust
of comfort bread.

Dead Men

The journey was calm
the need to honour
the grave of his end

the silence of death
kissed away the pulse
and sucked clean the lungs
when the skin
now waxed white and cold
yet colder still to grow

the crisp flurry
whitened the living grass
soon to feed
on rotten flesh

and yet his being
once seen important
now housed in wood
restraining the dead
would be forgotten
as rolling centuries
came once more

Dead Woman's Daughter

The way you looked
with sunken eye
let me know
and feel the dread
to see you in her guise

for she and I loved
as man to woman
no brothers we
with thoughts disdained

but oh the fire
wanted to keep
religion of life
spring the hill
to wax and wane

and as in all
it came to us
to die as one
but it was not

she in illness fell
her stomach taken
by the scuttling
of no kind crab

but oh our bonny find
the love the gape
was ours
and never may
I see her now
but in this child of mine

Ebb

And now the end
the left lying man
winced as the song
of his breath
warbled and waned

the flowers were beautiful
the pride of a garden
scented and warm
with colours of red
and no angry hue

the river flowed on
its banks eroded
the years had formed
a winding way
a melody of water
that gurgled with relief

First Flame

And so they have come
with green umbrellas
blown inside out
beads of water
running off
the foliaged fabric

and each day I look
to find the first
orange or red
carried high
above the leaves
like the throat of a flame

For I am all of Death

I creep behind
the shadows of life
and find sadness
seeping through minds

I have seen
flecks of pain
bloody kissed lips
and hastened death

for I am all of death
and every life
shall know
and curse my kind

let valleys ring
with the din of Hell
and the clamour for Heaven
when death is the tale.

God of Humanity

A lemon scented fairy tale
the floss of fairground fun
a star bird calling willow
a teardrop wets the sun

the smell of burning corn
a lapwing all but done
the tiny moth of freedom
a spotted cheetah's run

an old bow and an arrow
a killer fires the gun
a scourge on humanity
God's work is never done.

Gone

The slim headed man
with you on his breath
bobbed up and down

you tried to give life
but he was too far gone

no pinking in him
the dinghy floated by
and you were lost
with no cry

I heard about it
when darkness came
and told you were gone

I cried my tears
on your pillow
wishing want not song

Guilt

That this demiorb
should light the marbelled way
and hang slack chained
as if to say
I am here and here
is eternity

watch unseen the air
that fills my chamber
full and frequent changing
and oh I am knowing of
he who hangs beyond
with chains the tighter so

he must be guilt
for guilt weighs heavy
and tightens sore

He Lives to Die

Twenty four hours
the happenings of a day
a day when the mayfly
kisses sunlight first
and packs life with all
for none shall come again

but this delicate wing
knows not of time
would he exchange flight
so short an ecstasy
for the curse of human years
I think not

so content to fly free
the pinnacle shall come
felt in the recess of survival
when gloriously to mate
he lives to die

Hellebore

It was beautiful
this paper thing
this light of joy
this wax of wonder

plucked from its nodding
away from the wind
and deluging rain
so perfect in whiteness

short stalked
it lay in the saucer
one stalk and a petal
bathed in water

I Die in the Beauty of Crowds

I die in the beauty of crowds
as the yellow streamers flutter
and dance in the garden of God
where blue balloons struggle
to break the string and the thought
that anchors to the gate of heaven

what word now great giver?
must I befriend you so that I
may lie snug on a bed of clouds
what would you have of me?
my life that you already know?

speak words I understand
who would have thought
that the mighty giver of life
might not communicate words
but grunt like a porcine
while the Devil bellows

to die as so and find it out
barred to go back and boast
to tell it all and show it so
where were the words of men
when you created swine
and curled their tails about.

If I Ever Should Fall

Who will be there?
when shadows long do fall
the living light does falter
and heights of heaven call
will you be there?
your love for me recall
my dear you must be near
if ever I should fall.

In the Grey Shadows

You did not see me
in the grey shadows
of my quiet place

I whispered your name
but you did not hear
as you prayed
kneeling by the bed

I heard you ask the Lord
to let him see his father
in the dust gathered years
before the angel came

then you looked
and saw me quiet
in the grey shadows
of my dying place.

It is my Time

Speak softly
as you kneel
it is my time
I would have it so

pray for me a little
thankful for love
and laughter
not hate nor shame
the silent ones

I wanted no more
than given
the dust gathered years
saw you by my side
and I am content.

Leaf in her Hand

She took the season
with wetness on her back
and fell among pine trees
out on Western Ridge

a jumble of a man
whistled her over
to stroke a kind thigh
until the brow of the hill
swallowed the sun

and stars came out
as they lay in a bosom
for they were lovers
paired in a bond
his leaf in her hand

Leaf with Broken Stalk

I gathered leaves
by the summer sun
fading now in warmth

the breakfast bar
covered in crumbs
her hair brush
bristled by

young Toby in his cot
full of gurgles and play

and there I saw
the slim face
grotesquely blue

she dangled on
till they cut her down
a leaf with broken stalk

Light of Love

And should this thing
called love come in
other ways to be blessed
and cherished
like frosted starlite night

to gaze and wonder
a trillion lighted specks
their shining starting
years ago

ah this is love
this is light
the light of the universe
the light of love

Love of their Naked Parts

Shall we say of them
they were once part of us
a part that childlike
saw foolish days
when there was meaning
in singing and chanting
that made life more secure

for then they were vulnerable
to the man called John
who would sneak up
without letting them see badness
the sweets would taste nice
but then he would hold hands
and take them behind the bushes

never tell their parents
he would find out if they did
and nightmares would come
as they did anyway
and so it went on
his love of their naked parts

Martini Song

And so it was said
by the martinied man
who rested on the arms
of his two bit queen

"love and liquor
will never die
they court the poor
and prosper the rich
sweet is their song
those able friends

they waltz in time
to the rigmarole
on a baudy beach
and clasp life's fools
to kill and maim"

My Dear Boy Don't Cry

Think of me now
when the lambs lie alone
when the mothering ewes
see their children all gone

the sadness of parting
like lambs with their woe
don't let them pretend
I wished you to go

for all the days gone
and all the days nigh
shall never replace;
my dear boy don't cry.

My Dying Star

But what if I saw you
in the sadness of my song
when the lemon scented sun
kissed the day and all its wrong

would you hold me and kiss me?
would you cry away my pains?
for you were all my stars
and the dust of you remains

deep the boring pain of it
the healing moon too far
to kiss away the crab
and save a dying star.

My Father's Star

My father's star
gave light
and shone after
his burning ceased

though long gone
such constance
willed strength
and nurtured being

his mantle was proud
but he never reached
the track side
where now I stand

I miss his love
his need to cheer
and sweep clean
my childhood

Never There Had Been

Let me go back
where a family was one
with children at my feet
the curse of life
was softer then

they laughed and cried
my pride to be a father
to one nay two

oh I worshipped their
child like ways
their boisterous being
their young lives
their love for me

but now I am horribly old
my body aching weary
a distance far from
the little ones

I journey with the thought
it was better I had seen
the tenderness of that time
than never there had been.

No Life in Him

Too soon too soon
a life is over
and the procession
calm and sedate
shall walk slow stepped
to a silent grave

there lifted turf
gives way to earth
and its space
and slowly slowly
the wooden restraint
is lowered to lie
on the floor of the earth
and then symbolic
the patter patter of dirt
on the screwed down lid

he within knows naught
of this timely act
he has seen with others
but now it is him
soon to give life
to flower and fauna
when no life in him.

Of Cat and Kin

I have seen lions
lick wounds
from buffalo
and bush pig

that such domination
be humbled
and yet the intestine eater
frightens the plains

a killer of many
to feed nations of cubs
who crawl toward
warthog holes
watch their birther
bring down the grunters

the squealers sacrificed
in the dawn light
chewed and eaten
bloody warm
to satisfy the hunger
of cat and kin.

Passage to Interment

Death came once more
to Mormond Hill
as men struggled
slippery under foot

the scene before
midwinter and bleak
the lacquered wood
rested upon me for
the time it took
to recover breath

I lay between
horse and deer
and on the ridge
the captain's lodge
where roasted carcass
feasted drunken men

timely they lifted
the struggle once more
to gain the flat peak
with welcome descent
the road to Rathen
and interment below.

Prosody Comes Late

Tomorrow has no thought
as it lies sleeping
sleeping in the womb
timely soon to be here
as yesterday becomes
the day now seen

and what of all the days
that have gone by?
stretching back time
gone with hours and days
when love and laughter
stood for happiness
hate and shame for blame

no time to wait
this measure of sun
moon and stars
a conundrum of chaos
beyond doggerel days
when all shall versify
and prosody come late.

Sleep and the Half Sleep

The afterthought of half sleep
when a honeycomb of thoughts
soothes the mind stretched by day

it is twilight not dark nor day
yet it must slow the brain
to unravel the peace of sleep

no one knows when sleep comes
the senses are quiet before
the ether creeps smoothly
intoxicates the prostrate state
and lets Morpheus be mindful
of bodies now vulnerable

half of sleep is death
a glimpse of self
beyond the grave.

Summer Over

Dry eyes groaned for tears
summer over she would not see
the brown brimmed hat again
the one he wore on Sundays
when he came to tea

all day Monday she recalled
the scent of apres rasage
the kiss on her hair
the touch on her breast
and the release of sexuality

she met him in Buenos Aires
a lover full of Latin life
seasoned by women
he gave all she wished

Juan looked up from the newspaper
dear faithful and boring Juan
"Camilla saw you in Buenos last week
- she said you were with a man
but I knew she was mistaken"

Tendon of Life

The tendon of life
was stretched
muscles flexed
nerves jangled
decapitation delivered

limbs blown ragged
viscera cheaply spent
blood blasted dirty
in the dying dust

sudden death
served the lucky few
better than pain
better then shock
better than burning

the hell of their living
worse than
the cusp of death.

The Agony of Flesh

Some substance to it all
but no tide shall turn
until the signal molten
splashes skin
to burn bone

scream the hurt of it
but bear the soul
to leak and drip
on the metal floor
only then we know
if the worker cares
to live or die

life means sucking
the milieu intérieur
and death well if
the larval flow
increases several fold
his soul will leave
the agony of flesh.

The Brown Season

You were in bed
in the shower or drying your hair
when I walked on dewed grass
the smooth soled shoes
where slipping on the slope
I nearly fell down
but turned it into a running
descent to stop a fall

starlings spooked
from the giant birch
swayed pulsing in a trance
I knew not how it was
they did not collide
but knew it mattered not

it grew cold and Autumn
cast off my long coat
and spurned me with his
damp chill
until retreat took me
to the warm fire

The Jericho Years

The Jericho years
were pains in my head
they straddled the good times
with worse times instead

they called for my freedom
they winced when I cried
God did not deliver
and all of me died

it was always forever
and all life was sad
the voice of me singing
and all that was mad

but mad was the song
that sang in my head
the truth of my being
was all of me dead.

The Language of Seasons

Black bruised black
the boots lie bovine
in a pool of stories
laced up the middle
tongued to speak

long faced
like a sickle moon
the frost of winter
gripped in a vice
that lies metal cold
in the silent shed

expectant summer
yawns through spring
the milk of sunrise
subdued in tomorrow
but willing to mellow
for the sake of today.

The Puppeteer

How timely small the life
that keeps the soul warm
and gives such pain
for all with lesser pleasure

the puppeteer tweaks
and dances our bodies
the music he alone hears
till time the curtains close
the audience gone
the puppet folded gentle
cased with care

forgotten to lie
in the attic of silence
where senses molder
and alert no more
to worldly fears.

The Purest Form

Beauty is seen
in the three of a triangle
and the fourness of a square
and in the circle where
infinity surely dwells

mathematically pure
until man turned
them into shapes
to see and use
since when they
be pure again

let us devise then
the purest form
that no man
can corrupt
and shape
to common use

The Song of Hearts

The kiss of daylight
unburdened the moon
and robbed the sky
of all the stars

a zephyr refreshed
the sleeping mind
and opened the eyes
of the verse man

he brushed his hand
over the dewy grass
felt its cool
and touched its wet

today would bring
the lilac lady to his pen
and the song of hearts
would thus be told

The Touch

Never before
the warm smoothness
of touching hands

never orchestrated
nor planned
but good

the risk of flesh
the feel the need
the wish the warmth

to touch again
the thought burned
and thrilled
minds to explore.

This Time in their Lives

A sunlit gull flew by
with Summer on its back
bound for a cooler ocean
the drone of angry mowers
cut the long grass

it was too hot to fish
but they were easy
their day long
together in friendship

they watched an otter
dance and roll
the moor hens squabble
and the dainty sticklebacks
wary of trout mouths

then it was over
time to follow the dying sun
touching the bracken moor
across three fields
and homeward won

Two Whispers

January
like two whispers
shakes Monday's ache
with cold and want

the wind asleep
dreams sweet
of zebra skies
and lemon storms

the yellow sea
laps the sand
red leaves more
than an angry sun

Under My Soul

Come under my soul
it will not be long
before the emptying
of good cheer
greys the colour of my skin
and congeals the blood
that flowed for miles
with life and love

ah love that knocked
that warmth of feeling
passioned rosy red
the need of everyone
to be caught in the storm
that rages day and night
to torment and salve
the willing want of men.

Undone

Undone
she wanted some song
to rid her of it
but no song came
and she watched turtles
scurry on the beach
with slim chance of survival
beyond lay an ocean
the scent on the breeze
told the silence
to come again
and see Wilberforce
the slave of children

Unspeakable Love

Orange you lay on the floor of your dreams
warm thoughts for Alfred a Lord it seems
the red coat that cloaked the hue of your hair
custodian come lock up all sinners beware

so gentle the boy you loved him so well
your dreams are all gone now people don't care
hard labour broke spirit and all of your dare
the ballad of Reading do all men not care?

now all is gone you shall exile in France
sad love was blighted and withered away
dear Oscar so tragic for love you did pay
unspeakable love the Victorian way.

Water has no Shape

Water has no shape
it must be contained
it may run in the brooks
the streams and the rivers
fill the clouds and seas
but it has no shape

flatness an infinite area
without inclination
lets water spread
to form a single
molecule thick skin
each held to the other
yet separate within.

Winehouse

And slowly I
sink into the wineglass
and hear her
back to black

her and her song
love is a losing game
who is her guy
her lover her fella?

she guts out the song
her drugs her living
her love
my wine in her glass

Winter Way

Darkness bludgeons by
in the winter of recess
and clings about
like a shabby cloak

the cold crop
chills the bony flesh
to grip and gouge
the eye of dawn

softly she returns
come death of light
when the clock
clicks round
to tell the afternoon
that night is nigh

so precious light
that parts the two
and lets us view
the wakened world

Woman

The sweet kiss of tomorrow
came with hope
for the woman
with naught in her head

men with no eyes
sat in the corner
drinking pale wine
from the gathered grapes
and the calamine tea
lay in their stomachs
and cried for the end

and she died
in the silver hall
in lavender lace
dreams all gone

and the sighing stream
gurgled with love
in a yellow ravine

Yassa Arafat

Orange and blue
the blessed bird of death
flew for his blood
the man who swore
at Israel
for one last time

this angry man
vehement for many
killed for his kind
and courted the flag
of freedom
free men of France

his old song
now dead opens
a window of hope
for his people
and the healing
of a Middle East sore.

Lightning Source UK Ltd.
Milton Keynes UK
25 August 2009

143070UK00001B/16/P

9 781848 761391